MY (MoneY) SYSTEM:
CHECKBOOK BUDGETING

Pay All Your Bills and Have More
Money Between Pay Periods!

ANDRÉA L. ALFRED

iUniverse, Inc.
New York   Bloomington

iUniverse books may be ordered through booksellers or by contacting:

iUniverse
1663 Liberty Drive
Bloomington, IN 47403
www.iuniverse.com
1-800-Authors (1-800-288-4677)

Because of the dynamic nature of the Internet, any Web addresses or links contained in this book
may have changed since publication and may no longer be valid. The views expressed in this work
are solely those of the author and do not necessarily reflect the views of the publisher, and the publisher
hereby disclaims any responsibility for them.

ISBN: 978-1-4502-2362-1 (sc)
ISBN: 978-1-4502-2363-8 (ebook)

Printed in the United States of America

iUniverse rev. date: 06/17/2010

Table of Contents

Dedication

This book is dedicated to the working people of the middle class who scrimp and scrape just to live from paycheck to paycheck. We are undoubtedly a vast majority of the world's workers today.

To God (the Universe) the Source of all that I AM, the active power in my life that seeded my mind with this system in my time of need.

To my mother, Laura Elizabeth Turnbull-Alfred, my father, Clement Beonard Alfred, and my Toni Nichole; may their souls live on in peace. To all of my sisters: Laura, Gaynell, Pamela, Virginia, Alfreda and Donna. We all share our spirituality, common sense and a good work ethic, which we received from our parents, ancestors and the universe.

To my beautiful daughter Loren, if not for her presence in my life I would not have the joy that I experience daily; you are my inspiration.

Thank you, thank you, and thank you!

Preface

This book describes a basic money-handling skill and is not a financial-advice book. You won't find any information or advice on how to invest, buy stock, purchase a home, etc. The bottom line about financial-advice books is that they are written for people who already have money and want to make more of it. However, the majority of the world's people (the working poor) struggle to keep enough money to have the basic living necessities for survival: food and shelter.

This system is simply a guide that can support those who are working daily but are barely able to make ends meet. It is useful for young adults who did not have someone to teach or show them by example how to handle their financial obligations. Today, given the state that our economy is in, this book is for everyone!

Introduction

MY (MoneY) System: the title of this book comes from taking the first and last letters of the word "MoneY," which equal "MY." Throughout this book it will be shown as MY System. This system is one that can assist you in having more money after your bills are paid and, most importantly, help you get from one payday to the next without being broke in the interim. Below is a short story about why and how this system was started. Later chapters will show you how to do it yourself.

In the early 80s, I was having serious money problems and could never keep up with a budget. I tried budgeting, but to no avail, as it did not keep me from overspending, which meant I didn't have money left over for myself nor enough to pay all my bills. However, I always kept a sharp eye on my bank account along with an impeccable checkbook register. This system solved the problem by helping me keep (kind of a) budget, by coinciding it with my checkbook register. MY System is one way to manage your money and your bills all in one place: your checkbook register. That is why it is named My MoneY System: Checkbook Budgeting.

Most people agree that these days, you are pretty much blessed if you have a job at all! (Thank you, Universe!). Our economy is in shambles and our deficit is utterly ridiculous. If our personal deficits were as bad as our government's, none of us would be creditworthy. It makes you wonder how they can get away with it when we can't. Nevertheless, in this society, everything you need to survive successfully depends on your credit score. Employers check your credit – so it can hinder your ability to get a job – credit is checked by apartment complexes, telephone companies, electricity providers, automobile dealerships, insurance companies, etc. The list goes on, and the bottom line is...

Good credit is important for successfully managing your financial responsibilities in today's economy.

Up-To-Your-Neck Debt

Eighteen years ago, I was reading a metaphysical book and in it was a line that went something like this: "I've been broke, but I've never been poor. Being broke is a temporary situation; being poor is a state of mind." The line was written by Mike Todd, it made a lot of sense to me, so I memorized and repeated it often. It gave me a sense of calm throughout my personal financial storms, until one fateful day in 1987, when I came to a hard realization: **I was tired of being broke!**

My first job was in 1976 at McDonalds when I was 17 and a senior in high school. The minimum wage back then was $2.30 an hour. After graduation, I moved to Houston, Texas, and briefly attended The University of Houston, Downtown. My first real job was in 1978 working at an insurance company as a computer tape librarian; my starting salary was $7,200 a year. A few years later I was now married and pregnant, and in August 1981, I gave birth to a beautiful baby girl I named Loren Genienne. By the time I left my first job in 1982, my salary was $10,800. From 1982 until 1985,

I was working as a personal lines insurance rater, at the end of that employment I was making $12,000 a year.

In the third quarter of 1985, I started working as a customer service representative for personal lines at a general insurance agency, with an initial salary of $13,020. At the same time we were having marital discourse which was plagued by financial problems but most importantly; I was not happy. I decided it was time to get out, so I did just that, I was now a single mother of a then 6-year-old daughter. I was not receiving child support on a consistent basis and the basic living expenses were eating up money faster than I could make it.

Strictly out of necessity, two years later, in 1987, I put MY System down on paper. However, the most important thing about those times was that I was happy, despite the fact I was always broke. My determination to provide for my daughter and myself was the driving force that brought this system into fruition. I would not compromise on my most important requirement: to provide my daughter and myself a nice place to live. There was no questioning the fact that my major expense would be renting a place that met my strict standards of security and cleanliness. To find something like that, which I could also afford, meant that I had to move further out to the suburbs of Houston.

In the spring of 1986, I moved to North Houston off I-45 and FM1960. At that time the neighborhood was considered way out of town. Good, dependable transportation was a necessity for getting back and forth to work. At that time, I was working in the Galleria area, now called Uptown. I had no credit at the time, but I did have my first car: a paid-off 1973 green Mercury Cougar that my dad co-signed for me in 1980. With such a long commute to and from work, the eight-cylinder Cougar was breaking down on a regular basis and using increasing amounts of money for maintenance and gas. Ultimately I had to add onto my list of expenditures a reliable mode of transportation. Yikes; a car note! I was told (to my disappointment) by the new car salesman I didn't have enough credit at that time to purchase a new car, so a used-car salesman exchanged my Cougar for a brown 1982 Datsun 210. It ran well and had much better gas mileage than the Cougar, which was a good thing with my long commute.

After getting approved for the Datsun, I was surprisingly then approved for several retail credit-card accounts. Most of you would not be familiar with some of the retailers since they are local and some are now out of business. I acquired Palais Royal, Sears, Sakowitz, and Montgomery Ward accounts. I used them to buy clothes, appliances and car maintenance. I knew I was up-to-my-neck in debt and slowly going down; I was caught up in a riptide and in order to survive; I had to keep swimming.

It wasn't long afterwards that it turned out the car maintenance became my largest debt with Montgomery Ward and Sears. The Datsun, after only a year and a half, was beginning to fade fast. The car was diagnosed with some kind of motor problem that, if not repaired, would mean it could no longer run. The costs to repair the problem would be more than the car itself was worth. On top of that, I had to ride around with a bag of fuses in order to start the car whenever I turned it off. I returned the car to the same car dealership where I purchased it and traded in the troublesome Datsun for a 1985 Ford Mustang, which I promptly named Sally. I held my breath and prayed that the dealership would not find out about the major motor work the Datsun supposedly needed, which I'm guessing now they probably already knew about when they sold it to me. Mustang Sally was a good-looking car at the time, but the car note was a bit higher than the last. I was continually dodging bill collectors, who harassed me at home and at work. My credit took an even harder blow and I was drowning in debt. Nevertheless, I diligently paid what I could, when I could.

To help stretch the little money left over after paying rent daycare and bills. Our meals at home consisted mostly of the same things week after week; grits and eggs, spaghetti, fish sticks with french fries and a vegetable and in the winter; chili. I never had enough money to grocery shop for food that lasted for one full week, I'd stop by the grocery store after work at least three or four times a week. The worry and stress of it started hitting me hard physically and I was soon diagnosed with a stomach ulcer. I contributed the ulcer to my bad eating habits and not having an appetite due to worrying about my financial stability. Luckily I had medical insurance coverage, but the prescription medications were too much of a financial hardship for me to continue them, so I started drinking aloe vera juice instead. I figured that if aloe could heal cuts and scrapes outside the body; it should do the same inside the body. The aloe juice worked wonders and my ulcer eventually went away in about six months. I must add; I also believe the ulcer was the Universe's way of telling me something had to give. I needed my health in order to support my daughter so I was forced to come up with a way to handle my finances for my health and wellness.

I was determined not to give up living in a nice place, so I desperately needed a better solution. Peace of mind was also important, as I simply could not handle any extra stress on top of everything else. I had to put some kind of order to the mess I made before it could get any further out of control. So, in early 1988, I implemented MY System. I did not know; back then that there was such a thing as a credit score and I had no idea what mine was at that time. I only knew I needed to make more money for the necessities of living and raising a child along with paying my bills on time to achieve the status of good credit.

On top of everything that was going on financially, medically and emotionally, in June 1988, my employer informed us that he was closing the Houston office. The agency was purchased by another agent and, luckily for me, they kept me on as the receptionist. While answering phones, I had plenty of time to study for the exam to get an insurance solicitor's license, which was required in order to move up. Afterwards I was promoted to a personal lines customer service representative position and received an increase in salary; in 1991, I was making $21,600 a year, plus commission. In August 1992, the agency downsized and began layoffs; I was unemployed for eight months.

During this layoff period I rarely went out due to my lack of money. My entertainment consisted of me and a few girlfriends, along with our kids, getting together a few weekends to play cards. Sometimes we would pack up to stay the night as we would play cards into the wee hours of the morning and get up the next day and cook big meals that we'd all contribute to purchase and everyone pitched in with the cooking and the cleaning up afterwards. This is where my daughter picked up the reputation of being a "big eater". The food on her plate was as much as was on mine; she'd eat it all and ask for seconds. She was probably happy to not have grits and eggs, spaghetti and fish sticks. Those good times shared with friends brought a lot of laughter into my life and helped me get through those tough times by keeping my mind off of my financial problems.

I found another job in March 1992 as an automobile insurance underwriter. The starting salary was less than what I was making before, at $19,200 a year. I had no choice but to accept it because it was better than not having a job; plus, unemployment was barely paying my rent. The layoff had set me back, and it took two years before I was making $21,000 a year again, which sunk me back down in debt.

To avoid the bill collectors I purchased a used answering machine for my home phone; in order to screen my calls. A short while later I started receiving calls on my new job from one of my most notorious bill collectors; this particular guy would call me almost every day at work. I'm guessing he was upset that he wasn't able to contact me at work for the past 8 months since I was laid off, and I never answered my home phone unless I recognized the person calling. I avoided his calls at work by asking our receptionist to screen my calls and tell him I was away from my desk or on another line. I knew I'd have to talk to him sooner or later due to me receiving numerous calls as part of my job description; to provide quotes to various agents. On this particular day he managed to get through as our regular receptionist was out sick. He was extremely rude to me when I told him I didn't have any money to send them. I advised him I was not going to lie to him and tell him I would send a payment; when I knew I didn't have it. The collector then threatened to garner my wages, we argued back and forth over that issue; he even told me that he would have me arrested. I began crying and hung the phone up; cutting him off. Evidently my boss overheard the conversation and called me into his office to discuss what was happening. I explained to him the situation with the collector. He advised me that there were rules that collection agencies had to abide by, which at that time I didn't know existed. He told me what to tell them and no more than fifteen minutes later that same collector called me again and I informed him to please stop calling me at work (one of the rules). It took me telling him not to call me at work at least three times; before he finally hung up on me.

Because I was naive back then about my rights as a consumer; I'm including some information that will be helpful for you to know. The Federal Trade Commission (FTC) the nation's consumer protection agency enforces the Fair Debt Collection Practices Act (FDCPA), which prohibits debt collectors from using abusive, unfair, or deceptive practices to collect from you. I have included a short list of practices that are off limits for debt collectors. It starts off with the rule which I used on my harassing collector. You can find more facts about debt collection rules at: http://www.ftc.gov/bcp/edu/pubs/consumer/credit/cre18.shtm

A debt collector may not contact you at inconvenient times or places, such as before 8 in the morning or after 9 at night, unless you agree to it. And collectors may not contact you at work if they're told (orally or in writing) that you're not allowed to get calls there.

Harassment. Debt collectors may not harass, oppress, or abuse you or any third parties they contact. For example, they may not:

- use threats of violence or harm;

- publish a list of names of people who refuse to pay their debts (but they can give this information to the credit reporting companies);

- use obscene or profane language; or

- repeatedly use the phone to annoy someone.

False statements. Debt collectors may not lie when they are trying to collect a debt. For example, they may not:

- falsely claim that they are attorneys or government representatives;

- falsely claim that you have committed a crime;

- falsely represent that they operate or work for a credit reporting company;

- misrepresent the amount you owe;

- indicate that papers they send you are legal forms if they aren't; or

- indicate that papers they send to you aren't legal forms if they are.

Debt collectors also are prohibited from saying that:

- you will be arrested if you don't pay your debt;

- they'll seize, garnish, attach, or sell your property or wages unless they are permitted by law to take the action and intend to do so; or

- legal action will be taken against you, if doing so would be illegal or if they don't intend to take the action.

Debt collectors may not:

- give false credit information about you to anyone, including a credit reporting company;

- send you anything that looks like an official document from a court or government agency if it isn't; or

- use a false company name.

- Unfair practices. Debt collectors may not engage in unfair practices when they try to collect a debt. For example, they may not:

- try to collect any interest, fee, or other charge on top of the amount you owe unless the contract that created your debt – or your state law – allows the charge;

- deposit a post-dated check early;

- take or threaten to take your property unless it can be done legally; or

- contact you by postcard.

Live and learn as the old saying goes, and experiencing the emotional stress of dealing with that particular collection agent was a lesson I had to learn for myself. I did not receive any more calls at work from that collector or any others as I advised them I was not allowed to accept personal call at my job. I could now work worry free knowing that bill collectors would no longer interrupt my work schedule; it felt as if the world had been lifted off of my shoulders.

The slow paying of my bills during the layoff period took its toll on my credit and my balances were getting way out of hand, to the point that I had no choice but to someway rein them in. I began searching for a consolidation loan to pay off my creditors; I filled out three different loan applications before I was finally approved. About six to eight months later, my credit recuperated enough for me to have enough positive credit to lease a house. It was very important to me to be able to provide my daughter a home with a yard. Everything was running smoothly as I paid off the consolidated loan and the up-to-my-neck debt was slowly going down enough that I could breathe again. I was consistently using MY System and everything was running smoothly. The bills were getting paid on time and my savings account was growing.

I began to receive more credit-card offers, and I accepted some, but I also began charging on the paid-off credit cards. I eventually forced myself to cut up the ones that I had paid off, since that was my ultimate weakness. MY System afforded me the ability to pay and handle the bills. Things were looking better and better, and everything at last; was working out well.

I finally reached the proverbial mountaintop by acquiring a major credit card! After that, I felt that I needed to make more money, so in March 1994; I left the $21K job for a position as a personal lines manager with a salary of $25K. During this time, I managed to save and pay down most of my credit responsibilities. In July of 1995, after only one and a half years, the Dallas-based company shut down our Houston department and I was laid off once again; this time I was out of work for six months.

During that layoff period I made sure I kept busy to keep my mind off worrying about not having a job. I missed a couple of car notes and was threatened with repossession. I had very little money for food so I tried to get food stamps but was denied because I was receiving unemployment and I had a car; which they informed me I would have to sell to qualify for benefits. I was upset and almost to tears when I asked to speak to a supervisor to whom I begged and explained that I did not want to apply for and remain on food stamps benefits; I only needed them just this one time. I was finally approved to receive emergency food stamp benefits; I was relieved that I could, at least, feed my child while I was laid off.

I looked for a job every other day. It was depressing to find that the jobs that were readily available were not paying enough to support my car and house notes alone; not including the other basic living necessities. So in the meantime, I painted the interior of my house on the days I did not look for jobs. I found bargains by purchasing only dented cans of paint from the local Home Depot, the dented cans were extremely marked down to unbelievably cheap prices that I could afford at the time. I also wrote poetry and joined a meditation group. Meditating with the group helped me tremendously by lowering my stress levels plus giving me someplace to go and get out of the house. I attended one night every week for a while and enjoyed the positive energy I received. One night after our meditation session was over I was surprised as the group offered me money to pay my car note to avoid repossession. I felt ashamed and told them I could not accept it. They insisted that I take it and added that they were glad they could help and advised me that I had no reason to feel ashamed, that I was led to the group for more than one reason. I have to admit that the group meditation helped me maintain a positive attitude by focusing and being grateful for everything I had; not on what I didn't have.

When I did not find a job paying what I was making before the layoff; I went back to work for one of my previous employers. The experience helped me understand that old saying: "You can't go back", is true, I was not happy, I could only stay there for two months. In February of 1996, I left and started working for myself on a commission-based salary as an insurance solicitor selling automobile liability insurance at used car dealerships. That only lasted six months before I began working in their finance department. The dealership closed a couple of months afterwards, and once again I found myself out of work – this time for a month before I found financial work at another dealership. After the bout of layoffs and salary changes, I had no choice but to rely even more on MY System. It helped me get through those rough times, but now I had money in savings and a positive credit rating.

In 1997, my daughter was turning 15 years old and in four years she would be going off to college. I started to worry about whether I had enough money for her college education. My prayers and hopes were answered in late February of 1997. I was referred by a dear friend, to apply for a position, which I received, at an organization that I continue to work for today.

Let me digress back to 1985, when I first started out on my own with my daughter and I in a small apartment off of FM1960. She was in kindergarten then. I would drop her off at daycare and tell her every week she had to make good grades in school so she could get a scholarship to go to college. There was no questioning of that rule; she was going to go to college, no matter what.

In early 2006, when I was laid off, I was watching a popular talk show and the subject matter was debt in this country. During the show it was stated that over 70% of Americans have serious debt problems — or in my own words, up-to-your-neck debt. I could relate, and for some reason I couldn't stop thinking about that show and their findings regarding the vast number of Americans who are in financial trouble and bogged down with serious up-to-your-neck debt.

I noticed that the majority of people who were featured on the debt show were married and had pretty decent incomes but still unable to handle their finances and obligations. At one point I actually got angry because when I was going through it I only had one measly income and was by myself, unable to rely on anyone else. Fortunately, my anger turned into pity, then from pity to wanting to help, that's when the thought of publishing MY System came to mind. I knew I had to share MY System with other people and show how it had worked for me, and I knew it would work for them too. It helped me get out of up-to-my-neck debt, and other people should know about it.

At first I was skeptical, telling myself that nobody wants someone else telling them how to handle their expenses and spend their money. Would people think it was too complicated? I was having doubts. Then shortly afterwards there was a follow-up show on the debt subject.

More than a few people admitted that they had never learned how to budget and pay bills and handle their finances. One of the reasons mentioned was not having anyone in their family set an example or demonstrate how to pay bills and manage financial responsibilities. It is not stressed enough in school how to individually manage your personal financial responsibility, nor are the consequences of a failure to do so. More now than ever, paying your bills in a consistent and timely manner; has become one of the most important processes of our credit-strapped society.

I do remember seeing my mother paying bills, writing out checks while lying on her bed. I would ride to the bank with her on numerous occasions. I didn't know what was going on inside the bank; I always had to stay in the car, and I would think to myself, I can't wait until I can go into a bank. We also made regular stops to the post office to mail bills and numerous personal letters. Additionally, I recall instances of when, instead of mailing our electric bill, we had to go directly to the electric company to pay them. I'm sure the reason was to get it in before the lights were turned off. So I did have an example of my mother paying our bills, but by the time I was old enough to have my own financial obligations; I did not have the know-how.

This guide is my way of setting an example for others who had no one to emulate. I'm happy to share how MY System works; I know it will help many people have the opportunity to ease the frustration of always living in a state of stress and anxiety, and develop the ability to pay the bills and to establish and maintain a good credit rating.

I can tell you factually that MY System has helped me get out of debt, move past collection harassments and finally establish a good credit rating. I hope this guide can be as positive a tool for you as it has been for me. I want this guide to be a part of helping to bring down that 70% of people who are drowning in up-to-your-neck debt. It's a fact that no one can continue living in a constant state of financial stress without it showing up physically or mentally, and always in negative ways.

Starting MY (MoneY) System: checkbook budgeting

If you want to do anything in life, you have to start out with a plan. I'm sure you're all too familiar with the term, "Timing is everything." It's something that rang true to me when I started MY System.

As I mentioned earlier, I devised the system months before I could actually start it. I put MY System on paper in early 1987 and I implemented it in the first quarter of 1988. I had to wait until I received my IRS tax refund, which I sacrificed in order to kick-start MY System. It was the only way to help get me out of the vicious cycle of either choosing not to pay bills in order to have money and food on the table, or paying the bills and not having any money for food, or much of anything else. You may not have to wait until you receive a kick-start like I did and if so, good for you. If your financial situations are anything close to what I experienced, then there is no better time than the present to start MY System.

STEP 1

LIST ALL YOUR BILLS

Write down in a list every bill that you have. I repeat: write down EVERY BILL that you have, making sure to include their due dates. Knowing when your bills are due helps you stay consistent with payments. Also, don't leave out other obligations like the beauty salon or nail salon if you go on a regular basis, and gas if you commute. These are bills, even though you don't pay them by mail. I have an example below:

List of Bills (Sample)

BILLs	DUE DATES
Rent/Mortgage	1st
Automobile	27th
Electricity	20th
Home Insurance	18th
Auto Insurance	24th
Credit Cards (2)	3rd & 10th
Telephone	5th
Gasoline	1st & 15th
Beauty Salon	5th
Water	24th

STEP 2

OPEN A CHECKING ACCOUNT

You probably have guessed by the title of this guide that one of the first things you should have is a checking account. This is your basic MY System tool. Most banks now offer free checking and savings accounts if you direct-deposit your paycheck. Besides, why would you want to give your money away by paying a check-cashing company or buying money orders? You've worked too hard for that money, why give it away? It may seem like a small amount to pay, but every penny, nickel and dime eventually adds up to dollars that you can use at your own disposal. If you do not have a savings account, open one for your backup cash.

STEP 3

Divide and Conquer

Once you have your list of bills and obligations, divide them in half and enter them into your check ledger as deductions. Splitting your bills in half each pay period will make a major difference with money on hand. Do that every pay period; either on the first and fifteenth, or every other week depending on your pay-period schedule. When I was on a first and fifteenth schedule of pay, I could adjust the deductions for the period that coincided with a particular bill's due date. Thus, some bills came out of the first pay period and some came out the fifteenth pay period. See my sample of a bill list below. (Please note that these are prices from the early 1990s.)

Total Monthly Bills		**Split Per Paycheck**
Monthly Rent	$400.00	$200.00
All Credit Cards (2)	$100.00	$50.00
Phone Bill	$25.00	$12.50
Water	$10.00	$5.00
Car Insurance	$75.00	$37.50
Monthly Car Note	$200.00	$100.00
Total	**$810.00**	**$405.00**

You are now taking out only half of your total bills per pay period, which leaves you with more of your paycheck for other purposes. Instead of a major deduction of $810 coming out of one paycheck, the smaller amount of $405 leaves you more money for other expenses. Once you divide the amount, deduct it from your checkbook ledger as if you were writing a check. By the time your bill is due, you should have half of the bill already waiting in your checking account.

On your next pay period, deduct the other half of the bill by writing a check for the full amount. I've included a sample of my old checkbook ledger (starting with my IRS kick-start) along with the meaning of some of the abbreviations for your information to keep up with other deductions from the account.

Checkbook Register Sample*

D	= Debt (1/2 bills)
CC	= Check Card Purchases
ATM	= Automatic Teller Machine (Cash Withdrawal)
TRAN	= Bank Transfers
DEP	= Deposit
X	= Item Has Cleared Bank

Item	Check Number	Date	Description of Transaction	C	Debit (-)	Credit (+)	Balance
1	DEP	3/11	Deposit IRS Refund	X		875.00	875.00
2	TRAN	3/11	Transfer to Savings Account	X	200.00		675.00
3	D	3/11	#1 - ½ Rent/Mortgage ($400.00)	X	200.00		475.00
4	D	3/11	#1 - ½ Car Payment ($200.00)		100.00		375.00
5	D	3/11	#1 - ½ Car Insurance ($45.00)		22.50		352.50
6	D	3/11	#1 - ½ All Credit Cards (1 @ $45 / 1 @ $55) ($100.00)	X	50.00		302.50
7	D	3/11	#1 - ½ Phone Bill ($25.00)	X	12.50		290.00
8	D	3/11	#1 - ½ Water Bill ($10.00)	X	5.00		285.00

	CC	Date	Description	X	Amount	Deposit	Balance
9	CC	3/13	Gasoline	X	10.00		275.00
10	1058	3/15	Groceries	X	55.12		219.88
11	ATM	3/16	Cash Withdrawal	X	20.00		199.88
12	DEP	3/31	Deposit Paycheck	X		700.00	899.88
13	1059	3/31	#2 – Hollister Apts. Rent (Paid $400.)	X	200.00		699.88
14	1060	3/31	#2 - Visa Credit Card (Pay $55)	X	25.00		674.88
15	1061	3/31	#2 - Master Card (Pay $45)	X	25.00		649.88
16	1062	3/31	#2 – Utility District #3 (Paid $10)	X	5.00		644.88
17	1063	3/31	#2 – AT&T (Paid $25.00)	X	12.50		632.38
18	ATM	4/01	Cash Withdrawal		100.00		532.38
19	DEP	4/15	Deposit Paycheck	X		700.00	1232.38

						Balance
20	TRAN	4/15	Transfer to Savings Account	200.00		1032.38
21	1064	4/15	#2 – Honda Financial (Paid $200)	100.00		932.38
22	1066	4/15	#2 – Allstate Ins. (Paid $60)	37.50		894.88
23	D		#1- ½ Rent/Mortgage ($400.00)	200.00		694.88
24	D		#1- ½ Car Payment ($200.00)	100.00		594.88
25	D		#1- ½ All Credit Cards (1 @ $45 / 1 @ $55) ($100.00)	50.00		544.88
26	D		#1 –½ Phone Bill ($25.00)	12.50		532.38
27	D		#1 - ½ Water Bill ($10.00)	5.00		527.38
28	TRAN	4/15	Transfer to Savings Account	200.00		327.38
29	DEP	5/1	Deposit Paycheck		700.00	1027.38

				Payment	Deposit	Balance
30	1067	5/1	#2 – Apartment (Paid $400)	200.00		827.38
31	1068	5/1	#2 - Visa Credit Card (1/2 of $50. Paid $45)	25.00		802.38
32	1069	5/1	#2 - Master Cards (1/2 of $50. Paid $55)	25.00		777.38
33	1070	5/1	#2 – Utility District #3 (Paid $10)	5.00		767.38
34	1071	5/1	#2 – AT&T (Paid $25.00)	12.50		754.38
35	D		#1 - ½ Car Insurance ($75.00)	37.50		717.38
36	D		#1 - ½ Car Payment ($200.00)	100.00		617.38
37	CC	5/5	Gasoline	30.00		587.38
38	CC	5/7	Groceries	48.13		539.25
39	TRAN	5/10	Transfer to Savings Account	200.00		339.25
40	CC	5/15	Dillard's	124.16		215.09

*Microsoft Corporation Check Register

I'm on a bi-weekly (every two weeks) pay schedule. The billing date payments are not as consistent as a first and fifteenth schedule. I put "No.1" and "No. 2" on the check register list, as they are halved closer to their consistent due dates. To make it easier to keep track of the deductions and payments, "No. 1" for the first half of a bill deduction and "No. 2" for the second half, or when the payment is made. Make sure you write down the amount that was actually paid out beside your description. See check #1059 (No. 2) – I'm writing the check for $400, but only deducting $200 on my account ledger because the other $200 has already been deducted from the first (No. 1) half of the rent /mortgage payments.

To make some bills easier to divide, you can take some bills that are paid out each month at a set amount and add them together. For example, in the sixth item from the top of the checkbook sample, you'll notice that my credit card payments are different; one is $45 a month and one is $55 a month, which equals $100. So in order to keep up with my written checks, I take out No. 1 of $50 (half of which is $25.00). But I pay those (items 15 and 16) with separate checks. However, I put down how much the check was for to the credit card company ($45 and $55) so I can keep track of the checks when they clear the bank to be able to identify them by the actual amount.

You can implement MY System in different ways, as long as you keep up with your documentation and account balance. Make sure that once a check for a bill has cleared your bank, you check off the first (No. 1) half of the deduction as well as the cleared check (No. 2). Not only are all my bills paid, but I have an additional $600 that will go into my savings account. Putting that extra money into a savings account is advantageous for you in the long run.

MY System relies on consistent logging in your checkbook ledger. This is very important, especially if you also use an ATM or check card. If you use a check card like I do, make sure to keep all your check card receipts (I put mine behind my paper money in my wallet), and at the end of a day or two you can deduct it from your checkbook register as ATM or check card (CC) purchases, just like you've actually written a check.

Back in the day, I used to check my bank balance on an every-other-day basis via telephone; now, the use of electronic banking allows you to go online or call into the customer service line to get balances and check items that have cleared the bank. It's also a good idea to check your bank account frequently when using an ATM or debit card to ensure that no one has gained access to your account number or check card.

The main point regarding using MY System is you don't have to keep a separate budget from your actual bill payments. This gives you the ability to keep correct account balances and a bill budget all in one place. It may take some time to acquire the flow of various bill's due dates. The longer you use the system, the better it will flow.

The Golden Rules

Always know your check account balance at the bank and in your checkbook ledger.

- Focus ONLY on the balance of your checkbook register, and keep up with deductions (not what you know is in the bank; this number can be off because of bills that are pending).

- Know when you can/can't afford it.

1). Utilize your bank's online website to keep up with your transactions. You should always know your bank balance. To balance your ledger, just deduct the amounts that have not cleared and/or that are still pending for bill payments No. 1 or No. 2.

2). When using MY System, remember that your bank balance will always be more than your checkbook ledger balance because all bills are not due at the same time. The most important thing to remember is: **do not spend the money already allotted to pay bills just because you know**

it is there. Always focus on the bottom line: the balance of your checkbook register. At least one half of your bills will always be in your account.

Only take emergency money out of your savings account. If you seem to be taking more money out of your savings than you should, then you need to start putting more money into your savings account. The best thing about MY System is that it will allow you to be able to put more money into your savings. You can always electronically transfer money into your checking account when needed. If you have a balance in your register showing $5 after you've deducted half of your bills and you need to use (let's say) $50 (knowing that $200 is there for half the rent) make sure you log the balance showing yourself in the red for -$45. When your next payroll or other deposits are made, you are back on track with the correct balanced amount.

3). The most important rule is this. If you do not have the money in the bank for something you want, simply tell yourself the truth: "I can't afford it at this time." Then save for it. It feels good to know that if any kind of emergency arises, you have some money in the bank.

Note: MY System does require some financial discipline, but if it helps you to pay your bills while saving money and building good credit, it's well worth it!

Divided Success

MY System was the ultimate lifesaver for me as I experienced all my employment and financial ups and downs. It worked for me then, and I still rely on it today. It's been twenty-three years, and I'm still using MY System. It took some time to recover my unsatisfactory credit ratings, but after a couple of years I was seeing light. I now have enough extra money to pay more than the minimum due on my credit cards (which is the only way to pay off credit cards). Using MY System will enable you to save more money for whatever reason, be it emergencies or major purchases. You must keep in mind that it will take time for your credit to heal if you had problems in the past. Ultimately, they will recover and you can purchase anything your heart desires.

In 1998, my positive credit rating allowed me to purchase my first home, which I sold in 2002. I purchased another home in May 2004 with 100% financing. I was able to re-finance after two years, which allowed me to comfortably afford a fixed mortgage. I consider myself lucky to get in on the great financing I received because shortly afterwards the bottom fell out of the real estate market.

While using MY System over the years, I managed to save money. I only hoped I had enough for my daughter's higher-education needs. However, she remembered my request and she did receive a partial college scholarship. MY System allowed me to save enough money to help with collegiate expenses for four years at McNeese State University at Lake Charles, Louisiana. I paid all the expenses that the scholarship did not cover, which was quite a lot more than I thought it would be! I didn't have enough savings to completely finance the entire amount and she ultimately received student loans to complete her courses, which were prolonged to get her master's degree. She moved back to Houston and found work. I'll admit she's also gone through her own financial disasters, and now also uses MY System. I'm happy to say MY System seems to be working for her in positive ways; she is now studying to get her Ph.D. from the University of Phoenix.

The most exciting thing MY System finally afforded me was peace of mind and good credit. I love taking advantage of the perks you can get with good a credit rating, and now I have it. I always took advantage of the furniture store's special sales when they offer no down payment, no payments or interest for a year. I've taken advantage of those offers more than a few times, and I've only purchased furniture through those kinds of sales. I'd simply save the money and pay it off before the year was up. However, you have to make sure you don't go overboard and purchase more than you can handle within the year's timeframe.

Recently I heard that due to the new credit card rules, the furniture stores can no longer offer no money down, no interest, no payment deals after February 22, 2010. At first I thought they may have stopped that type of finance offer due to the majority of people paying off their balances right before the year was up and the banksters (yes, just like gangsters) were not making money, so they had put a stop to it. I was wrong. The feds found too many cases of excessive fine print that misled customers and left them paying huge interest rates after the promotion time was up. Appliance and furniture stores say that it's the savvy customers, who use these programs the right way – like me, who will lose out. Too bad; it was a great way to purchase furniture and large ticket items.

Having good credit has also allowed me the ability to lease a car, something I always wanted to do. The main reason was recalling the nightmares of my old cars always breaking down, coupled with enormous car maintenance expenses. I know now that my car maintenance obligations were one of the largest contributors to my bad credit ratings. It still makes me uneasy when I think about it. Most leasing payments are lower than a purchase would be when buying a car. Additionally, since I'm a single woman who knows nothing about car maintenance, it makes me feel more secure to know that my car is always under warranty until the lease is up, and I won't ever have to worry about unexpected maintenance charges again. If my car does happen to break down, I just call the roadside assistance I received with my lease. You see, the dealership is really still the owner of the car, and they want to make sure it is taken care of. After the lease is up I turn it in and get another brand-new car all without maintenance worries!

My money-saving secret to car leasing is finding and using only one model of car that I like and staying with that particular car from one lease to the next, always using the same dealership. Returning to the same dealership helped me avoid the large down payments that are required. My first lease was in 2004, and the down payment required was $1,000. When I turned it in for another lease, they offered to give me the down payment due to me being a returning customer which means you're more likely to get a better deal with little or no down payment on a brand-new car lease. I understand that leasing a car is not for everyone, as most people like to think of owning their car after it's paid for. Buying, on the other hand, is a better choice if you want transportation without a car payment in the long run, or if you're considering the purchase of a used car. Since most of the depreciation occurs in the first few years after a car is built, leasing a used car may not save you money. Additionally, extra mileage costs must be considered when you lease, if you frequently make long trips, purchasing your car may be the way to go. But for me, after all my awful experiences with car troubles, it was just the opposite; I felt like the car owned me and the money in my bank account. Nevertheless, I accomplished my goal with the help of MY System. You can see immediately what a difference it makes not having large amounts coming out of one paycheck. Instead you are dividing all bills in half, giving you more money left over from each paycheck.

It was a long, hard ride to get here, and as you can see by the current list of my bills today, (included in this chapter) shows I no longer struggle with a measly salary. However, the more money you make, the more you spend, and the more you spend the more bills you acquire. I try to buy everything with cash now, and utilizing MY System for so long has afforded me that luxury. It feels good pay your bills and still have money left over for other necessities and savings.

Some of you may think that MY System uses too much of the checkbook ledger, and you are right. You may ask, why not just put it on paper and then deduct it? I do now put mine on paper first, then in my ledger, because I tend to lose and misplace papers. And yes, it does take up a great deal of the checkbook register. I now order extra checkbook registers, but back in my broke days I would go into the bank and ask for one or two, and they would give them to me.

Now, after using MY System for over 20 years, I no longer keep the list in my checkbook register, as I'm very accustomed to the flow and workings of the system. I'd suggest you do the same until you are familiar with the system and the flow of your bills. I'm so familiar with my bills that I only deduct the amount at the bottom of my bill list showing the total amount of $1,266.65 out of my checkbook balance after every pay period. I keep a copy of the bill list in my checkbook cover until all bills are crossed off a particular list. I also have the bill list saved in my computer, so I only have to change the first column numbers showing which half of the bill amount is coming out of the account for that pay period. I still use credit cards, but now can pay them down (paying more than the minimum due) within a shorter period of time. You'll soon find yourself happily taking bills out of the list as you pay them off!

You can take advantage of having more money in your checking account by switching from a regular checking account to an interest-earning checking account, since larger balances stay in the account. Now your checking account is making money too; granted, it's not a lot, but every little bit counts.

I've inserted below a recent list of my current bills to show how far I've gone on this system from 1989 to 2010. This is what my list of bills looks like now.

COLUMNS

Column 1	Number of Payment Deductions, 1st or 2nd half (No. 1 or No. 2)
Column 2	Name of Biller and Amount Due
Column 3	Bill Due Date
Column 4	Amount deducted (half amount due) from your account

#1	Credit Card (Home Maint. $50)	11th	$25.00
#1	Retail Credit Card (Pers. $50)	12th	$25.00
#1	Electricity ($200.00)	21st	$100.00
#1	Dental Credit ($161.00)	19th	$80.50
#1	Cell Phone ($57.45)	17th	$28.73
#1	Home Insurance ($82.51)	18th	$41.25/.26 (*)
#1	Cable TV ($80.88)	18th	$40.44
#1	Water ($34.00)	18th	$34.00
#1	Credit Card ($100.00)	15th	$50.00
#2	Auto Insurance ($147.65)	24th	$73.82/.83 (*)
#2	Credit Card Visa ($126.00)	2nd	$63.00
#2	Loan ($50.00)	1st	$25.00
#2	Home Phone ($44.19)	5th	$22.09/.10 (*)
#2	Car Lease (#382.77)	27th	$191.39/.38 (*)
#2	Credit Card ($100.00)	2nd	$50.00
#2	Mortgage ($778.84)	1st	$389.42
#2	Yard Maintenance ($54.00)	Every 2 wks	$27.00
	TOTAL FROM CHECKING		**$1,266.65**

I once worked with a girl who never logged in the cents in her check ledger; she always rounded up to the nearest dollar. Sounds good, but I'm a Virgo and I have to balance down to the exact penny.

In my list above, you'll notice some asterisks (*). They mean that the cents are to be used depending on whether it's the first or second half. Example: On the insurance No. 1, I added $41.25 because it was the first half of the bill. In the next pay period, when it will be the second half of that same bill, I'll add $41.26 for a total of $82.51; the amount due on the bill.

I have placed some blank pages at the end of the book so you can start listing your bills. I've also included a sample of a checkbook register for practice at dividing and conquering your way out of debt and finding yourself with more money in hand between pay periods. So let's get started on your own divided success.

Bill Listings

Notes

Bill Listings

Bill Listings

Sample Of Checkbook Register

Sample of Checkbook Registers for Your Use/Practice

Check Number	Date	Description of Transaction	C	Debit (-)	Credit (+)	Balance

Sample of Checkbook Registers for Your Use/Practice

Check Number	Date	Description of Transaction	C	Debit (-)	Credit (+)	Balance

Microsoft Corporation Check Register

Conclusion

We've all heard the saying "We are all one or two paychecks away from being homeless." It's scary but true, so think about it. How many pay periods can you miss before things start to unravel? So, in the meantime, while you are blessed with a job (as I am), make those paydays work for you!

My intention is to have MY System taught to young adults attending high school and college. I know it can be of value for anyone who works. I believe everyone should learn this financial self-help technique. Using MY System takes discipline and patience and a whole lot of "I can't afford it" statements, but it is well worth it; in the end.

As I've stated, I still use MY System. The ability to divide my total bills into the number of pay periods I receive is the secret to my financial freedom and good credit. I want it to be yours, so that you too can call it MY System.

If you have any questions or would like me to come to your class, business, or to help you with a one-on-one instructional session to explain MY System in greater detail, I would be more than happy to accommodate you. Send your request to andreaalfred@sbcglobal.net. I look forward to sharing this system with everyone so that you too can divide and conquer your way to financial freedom.

Love & Light,
Andréa L. Alfred

About the Author

Andréa Lynette Alfred was born and raised in Norfolk, Virginia. She is the youngest of six (all girls) in the Alfred Family. After graduating high school in Virginia Beach, Virginia, she moved to Houston and attended the University Of Houston, Downtown. She has one daughter, Loren Genienne Bryant and a grandson, Brian Christopher Price; and is lovingly known by him as G-Mama. She lives in Houston, Texas and is currently working as an office manager.